A

Pony Rider's

DIARY

This Diary Belongs To:

____

*19*___

A *Pony Rider's* DIARY

Nina Duran

PRENTICE HALL PRESS

New York □ *London* □ *Toronto* □ *Sydney* □ *Tokyo*

To Nona Garson,

my friend and trainer

who understands ponies

better than anyone I know

and to Popcorn . . .

Prentice Hall Press
Gulf + Western Building
One Gulf + Western Plaza
New York, New York 10023

A Prentice Hall Press Equestrian Book

ISBN 0-13-685470-2

Printed in Japan

10 9 8 7 6 5 4 3 2 1

First Edition

Contents

Introduction

Without fail, that first moment—when I'm going to visit my hunter at the farm or I pass a carriage horse in the park and just catch that horsey scent in the air—I'm always brought back to my Popcorn days. Popcorn permitted my first ride on a Saturday morning, with my brother and father watching. He was ancient and, looking back, unbelievably tolerant. Hanging onto his very full mane, I was bounced around the ring a few times, giggling with delight. He very kindly stopped at the gate, waited quietly while I was lifted off by my father, and proceeded to pin his ears flat on his head. He looked fierce, but I understood him perfectly. Out came a piece of sugar from my pocket, and his ears perked up. He got his thank you. From then on I was hooked.

Many of the world's outstanding riders got their start on a pony, taking endless turns around the ring trying to keep the pony from drifting toward the center (an invaluable, early lesson in leg aids), learning the art of perseverance on an animal that offers no shortcuts. Watching a seasoned pony carry its young rider, one senses that the pony is doing the teaching. With an uncanny sense of a rider's limitations and often genuine kindness, ponies seem to possess an intelligence you don't always see in horses.

Ponies also have a superior sense of balance, owing to their lower center of gravity, and pound for pound seem to be better athletes than horses. It is amazing to see a pony accomplish horse-size feats, and after riding horses for years now, I'm still amazed by how good ponies are.

They seem to come in two varieties. There are the wise, ancient ponies like Popcorn—the sage "belly splinter" ponies that tuck their legs up to their chin when they jump, ears pricked, taking care. They are the ponies that have taught the mothers and now carry the daughters, that keep moving often into their thirties, the only difference being that they are perhaps a bit more set in their ways. But, however stubborn, they remain unflappable, like Lancer, the flea-bitten gray who's taught nearly every-

body at my barn. He's impossible to flex or bend, but he knows the instructor's words by heart and canters on command, giving the rider a thrilling sense of accomplishment that may be false but still builds confidence.

Then there are the imps, the ponies who teach you the art of falling off ("That's yours now," the instructor would say, pointing to the patch of ground I'd landed on.) Pretty Boy was my first fall. And sweet Timmy, a tiny dappled gray, perks up whenever he sees a jump in front of him. He loves to go fast, and the rider who doesn't see his eyes suddenly go bright with anticipation will have a handful in a moment.

But there is a lovely little mare named Rosie at the barn who's the ideal. Neither an ancient nor an imp but a little bit of both, she's a quality pony who's taught her young owner kindness, courage, and a deep sense of responsibility. They adore each other. Rosie always gives her all and never misses in the ring, and her rider concentrates with a child's intensity. It's no wonder they've won so many ribbons. They're a beautiful picture.

— N.D.

My Pony's Vital Statistics

Registered show name ______________________

Stable ______________________

Breed ______________________

Color/Markings ______________________

Height ____________

Year of birth 19_____

Date of purchase ______________________

Sire ______________________

Dam ______________________

Insurance company/Broker ______________________

Policy number ______________________

Type of coverage ______________________

Insured value:

Pony ____________

Tack ____________

Renewal dates ______________________

Freeze mark number ______________________

▫ My Pony's Stable ▫

Name ______________________________

Address of stable ______________________________

Telephone number ______________________________

Stable owner ______________________________

Manager ______________________________

Instructors ______________________________

____

____

____

Grooms ______________________________

____

____

____

The People Who Look After My Pony

Groom (s) ________________________________

Telephone number(s) ________________________

Veterinarian ______________________________

Telephone number __________________________

Blacksmith _______________________________

Telephone number __________________________

My Pony's Feeding Schedule

Morning:

Type and quantity of feed ____________________

____

Hay (quantity) ____________________________

____

Afternoon:

Type and quantity of feed ____________________

____

Hay (quantity) ____________________________

____

Special instructions ________________________

____

____

____

Blacksmith and Veterinary Care

Blacksmith ______________________

Shoeing (Note dates pony is due to be shod):

January ______________ *July* ______________

February ______________ *August* ______________

March ______________ *September* ______________

April ______________ *October* ______________

May ______________ *November* ______________

June ______________ *December* ______________

Special care ______________________

Veterinary check / Treatment ______________________

Grooming and Stable Supplies

- ☐ *Dandy brush*
- ☐ *Body brush*
- ☐ *Water brush*
- ☐ *Curry combs*
- ☐ *Mane/Tail combs*
- ☐ *Hoofpick*
- ☐ *Sweat scraper*
- ☐ *Sponges*
- ☐ *Towels*
- ☐ *Fly spray*
- ☐ *Hoof oil*

Other items:

- ☐ *Liniment*
- ☐ *Wound powder*
- ☐ *Poultice*
- ☐ *Water buckets*
- ☐ *Shampoo*
- ☐ *Hay net*

My Pony's Tack and Clothing

Saddle ____________________

Size ____________________

Girth size ____________________

Bit (s) ____________________

Bridle/Martingale ____________________

Halter:

Size ____________________

Color ____________________

Stable rug:

Size ____________________

Color ____________________

Turnout rug:

Size ____________________

Color ____________________

Sweat rug:

Size ____________________

Color ____________________

My Riding Clothes

Helmet or hat size ______

Shirt:

Size ______

Color ______

Jacket:

Size ______

Color ______

Jodhpurs:

Size ______

Color ______

Boot size ______

Gloves:

Size ______

Color ______

My Riding Friends

Owner/Rider ____________________

Telephone number ____________________

Pony's name ____________________

Owner/Rider ____________________

Telephone number ____________________

Pony's name ____________________

Owner/Rider ____________________

Telephone number ____________________

Pony's name ____________________

My Favorite Riders
(and why I admire them)

Name ____

____

Name ____

____

Name ____

____

My Favorite Ponies
(and why I like them)

Pony's name ____

____

Pony's name ____

____

Pony's name ____

____

□ My Favorite Horse Stories, Books, and Films □

Title ______________________________

____

Title ______________________________

____

Title ______________________________

____

□ My Local Pony Club □

Name ______________________________

District ______________________________

Location ______________________________

Secretary's name ______________________________

Secretary's telephone number ______________________________

Instructor's name ______________________________

Instructor's telephone number ______________________________

My membership number ______________________________

Membership renewal date ______________________________

Annual events ______________________________

____

____

____

____

□ My Training Schedule □

*Instructor*____

*Things we worked on*_______________________________

*Things to practice on my own (and to remember)*______

▫ My Training Schedule ▫

Instructor ____

Things we worked on ________________________________

____

____

____

____

____

Things to practice on my own (and to remember) ______

____

____

____

____

____

My Training Schedule

Instructor

Things we worked on

Things to practice on my own (and to remember)

My Training Schedule

*Instructor*______________________________

*Things we worked on*______________________________

____

____

____

____

____

*Things to practice on my own (and to remember)*______

____

____

____

____

____

My Training Schedule

Instructor ________________________

Things we worked on ________________________

Things to practice on my own (and to remember) ________

My Training Schedule

Instructor ___________________________

Things we worked on ___________________________

____

____

____

____

____

Things to practice on my own (and to remember) ______

____

____

____

____

____

My Training Schedule

Instructor

Things we worked on

Things to practice on my own (and to remember)

My Training Schedule

*Instructor*____

*Things we worked on*________________________________

*Things to practice on my own (and to remember)*_____

My Training Schedule

*Instructor*________________________

*Things we worked on*________________________

*Things to practice on my own (and to remember)*________

□ My Training Schedule □

*Instructor*____

*Things we worked on*____________________________

*Things to practice on my own (and to remember)*____

Horse Show Checklist

Grooming equipment:

- [ ] *Dandy brush*
- [ ] *Body brush*
- [ ] *Water brush*
- [ ] *Curry combs*
- [ ] *Hoofpick*
- [ ] *Sweat scraper*
- [ ] *Sponges*
- [ ] *Towels*
- [ ] *Quarter markers*
- [ ] *Fly spray*
- [ ] *Hoof oil*

Braiding equipment:

- [ ] *Combs*
- [ ] *Scissors*
- [ ] *Rubber bands/Needles and thread/Yarn*
- [ ] *Step ladder/Stool*

Other items:

- [ ] *Water bucket*
- [ ] *Hay net*
- [ ] *Feed*

▫ Horse Show Checklist ▫

My pony's tack and clothing:

- ☐ *Saddle*
- ☐ *Pad*
- ☐ *Martingale*
- ☐ *Girth*
- ☐ *Travel bandages*
- ☐ *Leg bandages*
- ☐ *Halter*
- ☐ *Lead rope*
- ☐ *Lunge line*
- ☐ *Bridle*
- ☐ *Breastplate*
- ☐ *Tail bandage*
- ☐ *Crupper*
- ☐ *Brush boots*
- ☐ *Sweat rug*
- ☐ *Exercise blanket*
- ☐ *Roller*

My riding clothes:

- ☐ *Hat/Helmet*
- ☐ *Shirt (and stock or tie)*
- ☐ *Jacket*
- ☐ *Jodphurs*
- ☐ *Boots*
- ☐ *Gloves*
- ☐ *Crop*
- ☐ *Spurs*
- ☐ *Hairnet*
- ☐ *Rubber boots*

The Horse Show

□ The Horse Show □

My ASHA number ______________________________

Pony ASHA number ______________________________

Coggins test (date) ______________________________

Pony's height card ______________________________

□ The Horse Show □

---

*Judge(s)*____

*My trainer*______________________________________

*My division/classes*______________________________

*My performance*_________________________________

*How I feel I did (including things to work on)*________

The Horse Show

Judge(s)

My trainer

My division/classes

My performance

How I feel I did (including things to work on)

□ The Horse Show □

---

*Judge(s)*__________________________________

*My trainer*__________________________________

*My division/classes*____________________________

*My performance*______________________________

*How I feel I did (including things to work on)*______

▫ The Horse Show ▫

---

*Judge(s)*______________________________

*My trainer*______________________________

*My division/classes*________________________

*My performance*__________________________

*How I feel I did (including things to work on)*______

The Horse Show

---

*Judge(s)*____

*My trainer*______________________________________

*My division/classes*______________________________

*My performance*__________________________________

*How I feel I did (including things to work on)*______

The Horse Show

Judge(s)

My trainer

My division/classes

My performance

How I feel I did (including things to work on)

▫ The Horse Show ▫

____

*Judge(s)*_______________________________________

*My trainer*_____________________________________

*My division/classes*______________________________

*My performance*_________________________________

*How I feel I did (including things to work on)*________

▫ The Horse Show ▫

Judge(s) ______

My trainer ______

My division/classes ______

My performance ______

How I feel I did (including things to work on) ______

The Horse Show

Judge(s)

My trainer

My division/classes

My performance

How I feel I did (including things to work on)

□ The Horse Show □

____

*Judge(s)*_______________________________________

*My trainer*_____________________________________

*My division/classes*_____________________________

*My performance*_________________________________

*How I feel I did (including things to work on)*_______

____

____

____

____

____

____

The Horse Show

Judge(s)

My trainer

My division/classes

My performance

How I feel I did (including things to work on)

The Horse Show

*Judge(s)*____________________________________

*My trainer*__________________________________

*My division/classes*____________________________

*My performance*______________________________

*How I feel I did (including things to work on)*______

The Horse Show

Judge(s)

My trainer

My division/classes

My performance

How I feel I did (including things to work on)

▫ The Horse Show ▫

Judge(s)

My trainer

My division/classes

My performance

How I feel I did (including things to work on)

▫ The Horse Show ▫

Judge(s)

My trainer

My division/classes

My performance

How I feel I did (including things to work on)

▫ The Horse Show ▫

Judge(s)

My trainer

My division/classes

My performance

How I feel I did (including things to work on)

▫ The Horse Show ▫

Judge(s)

My trainer

My division/classes

My performance

How I feel I did (including things to work on)

□ The Horse Show □

____

*Judge(s)*____

*My trainer*____

*My division/classes*____

*My performance*____

*How I feel I did (including things to work on)*____

The Horse Show

Judge(s)

My trainer

My division/classes

My performance

How I feel I did (including things to work on)

□ The Horse Show □

____

Judge(s) ______________________________

My trainer ______________________________

My division/classes ______________________________

My performance ______________________________

How I feel I did (including things to work on) ______________________________

____

____

____

____

____

____

The Horse Show

Judge(s)

My trainer

My division/classes

My performance

How I feel I did (including things to work on)

The Horse Show

Judge(s)

My trainer

My division/classes

My performance

How I feel I did (including things to work on)

The Horse Show

Judge(s)

My trainer

My division/classes

My performance

How I feel I did (including things to work on)

□ The Horse Show □

____

*Judge(s)*________________________________

*My trainer*______________________________

*My division/classes*______________________

*My performance*__________________________

*How I feel I did (including things to work on)*______

____

____

____

____

____

____

The Horse Show

Judge(s)

My trainer

My division/classes

My performance

How I feel I did (including things to work on)

□ The Horse Show □

Judge(s)

My trainer

My division/classes

My performance

How I feel I did (including things to work on)

The Horse Show

Judge(s)

My trainer

My division/classes

My performance

How I feel I did (including things to work on)

The Horse Show

Judge(s)

My trainer

My division/classes

My performance

How I feel I did (including things to work on)

The Horse Show

Judge(s)

My trainer

My division/classes

My performance

How I feel I did (including things to work on)

▫ The Horse Show ▫

____

*Judge(s)*_______________

*My trainer*_______________

*My division/classes*_______________

*My performance*_______________

*How I feel I did (including things to work on)*_______________

▫ The Horse Show ▫

____

*Judge(s)*______________________________________

*My trainer*____________________________________

*My division/classes*_____________________________

*My performance*_________________________________

*How I feel I did (including things to work on)*________

____

____

____

____

____

____

The Horse Show

Judge(s)

My trainer

My division/classes

My performance

How I feel I did (including things to work on)

The Horse Show

Judge(s)

My trainer

My division/classes

My performance

How I feel I did (including things to work on)

The Horse Show

Judge(s)

My trainer

My division/classes

My performance

How I feel I did (including things to work on)

The Horse Show

Judge(s)

My trainer

My division/classes

My performance

How I feel I did (including things to work on)

The Horse Show

____

Judge(s) _______________

My trainer _______________

My division/classes _______________

My performance _______________

How I feel I did (including things to work on) _______________

The Horse Show

Judge(s)

My trainer

My division/classes

My performance

How I feel I did (including things to work on)

The Horse Show

Judge(s)

My trainer

My division/classes

My performance

How I feel I did (including things to work on)

The Horse Show

Judge(s)

My trainer

My division/classes

My performance

How I feel I did (including things to work on)

□ The Horse Show □

---

*Judge(s)*____

*My trainer*______________________________________

*My division/classes*______________________________

*My performance*_________________________________

*How I feel I did (including things to work on)*________

▫ The Horse Show ▫

Judge(s) ______________________________

My trainer ______________________________

My division/classes ______________________________

My performance ______________________________

How I feel I did (including things to work on) ______________________________

□ The Horse Show □

Judge(s)

My trainer

My division/classes

My performance

How I feel I did (including things to work on)

The Horse Show

Judge(s)

My trainer

My division/classes

My performance

How I feel I did (including things to work on)

My Ambitions with Ponies and Horses

This Is a Picture of My Favorite Pony

A Pony Rider's Diary

Composed in Caslon 540 Roman and Italic

Designed by Danielle Sacripante